as administrative centres for the lord's estates and as symbols of his power and position.

In England and Wales the 13th century was the apogee in the architectural development of the castle, culminating in the ruthless sophistication and massive strength of Edward I's castles dominating Gwynedd in north Wales. Whereas Scotland possessed no castles comparable in strength to Dover, Caerphilly, Caernarfon, Conwy, Harlech and Beaumaris, castle-building in the northern kingdom exhibited all the structural development associated with these great castles, as Caerlaverock, Kildrummy, Bothwell and others bear witness.

These developments, notably the systematic use of mural towers and the powerful gatehouses, were not new but they reached the height of their effectiveness in these years. The mural tower projected forward from the curtain wall of the castle to provide protection for the exposed outer face of the wall. The gatehouse was usually formed by two massive mural towers, one on either side of the entrance passage. With added drawbridges and portcullises, this potential weak-spot became the strongest element in the castle, often incorporating the best residential accommodation.

These castles showed their mettle in the Wars of Independence fought in the late 13th and the early 14th centuries. The wars revolved around the figures of Edward I (1272–1307), Edward II (1307–1327) and Edward III (1327–1377) of England and the great patriotic Scottish leaders, William Wallace (executed 1305) and Robert I (1306–1329), better known as Robert Bruce. There had been Anglo-Scottish wars before the reign of Edward I but their nature changed dramatically after his numerous campaigns. Between 1296 and his death at Burgh-upon-Sands overlooking the Solway on 7 July 1307, Edward exhausted his kingdom's resources in a ruthless but vain attempt to conquer Scotland. Despite his eventual epitaph, 'the Hammer of the Scots', his lack of finance prevented him from repeating his Welsh castle-building programme in Scotland.

FACING PAGE: *David I and his grandson Malcolm IV. David introduced Norman methods of government and became the most powerful 12th-century Scottish king. A pale shadow of his grandfather, Malcolm's appearance earned him the nickname 'the Maiden'.*

TOP: *A scene from a medieval manuscript showing labourers constructing a tower under close supervision.*

ABOVE: *This fine example of tower-house construction at Huntly dates from the end of the 16th century. (See page 32.)*

Nevertheless Edward I was able to capture all the existing castles in central and southern Scotland and garrison them with English cavalry who terrorized the surrounding districts into submission. He was also able to use his invincible cavalry squadrons in winning great victories like the battle of Falkirk (1298), but he was unable to extinguish the flame of resistance in Scotland, first lit by William Wallace in 1297 and then exploited by Bruce after 1306.

Edward I was leading yet another English army north when he died in sight of the country that had always eluded him. It left his great rival Bruce mismatched with his own weak and unwarlike son Edward II. While Edward languished at court surrounded by Piers Gaveston and his other favourites, Bruce consolidated his position in Scotland. He began reducing the lowland castles to his authority until by summer 1313 his forces were beneath the precipitous crags and walls of Stirling. Edward had made a feeble attempt to counter Bruce's power in 1310–11 but he clearly did not take the threat seriously until the Scots were besieging Stirling. He raised a massive army and rushed north at breakneck speed. Unfortunately Edward's generalship exhibited all the weaknesses and failings of his kingship and his army was routed at the battle of Bannockburn (1314). Bruce's great victory settled the question of Scottish independence for his lifetime.

The death of Robert Bruce in 1329 was the signal for internal conflict and a renewal of the threat from England where the character of the king had changed dramatically. Edward II had been overthrown by his own wife Isabella and her lover Roger Mortimer in 1327. He had been succeeded by his son Edward III who asserted his own authority three years later and was to prove one of the great military kings in English history. Allied to his inspired leadership was the invincibility of the English longbow. The latter was ruthlessly demonstrated at the battles of Dupplin Muir (1332) and Halidon Hill (1333). Scotland seemed at the mercy of the young and energetic

English king but his ambition knew no bounds and his attention was increasingly turning towards the fame and riches to be earned from military adventure in France. The result was the beginning of the Hundred Years' War (1337–1453).

The Anglo-Scottish wars continued intermittently and usually disastrously for the Scots until the accession in 1603 of James I, the first Stuart king of England. Amongst these battles were Neville's Cross (1346), Homildon Hill (1402), Flodden (1513), Pinkie (1547) and finally after 1603, Culloden in 1746. In the earlier part of the wars and only to a slightly lesser degree in the 16th century, the campaigns were dominated by the castles. They were the means of practical political power, with their garrisons being able to dominate the surrounding countryside and their effective defence out of all proportion to the number of men involved.

The campaigns of Edward I and Robert Bruce were largely a succession of sieges punctuated only infrequently by pitched battles, as at Bannockburn when the English army of relief encountered the besieging Scottish force on the flood plains of the Forth beneath the castle of Stirling.

It was the military genius of Robert Bruce that devised a successful strategy to wrest control of the Lowland castles from the English occupation forces. He initially made the same mistake as William Wallace by challenging English rule on the battlefield. The superiority of the English cavalry ensured their success in battle, as Wallace discovered at Falkirk in 1298, and Bruce eight years later at Methven. Thereafter Bruce resorted to a strategy of guerilla raids which weakened the supply lines of the English and left the castles vulnerable to Scottish attack. He also devised tactics to counter the supremacy of the English cavalry and these were strikingly vindicated at the battle of Bannockburn.

There were in Scotland castles other than great royal strongholds like Stirling and Edinburgh. Those usually built in the later Middle Ages were tower-houses. As the name implies, the tower-house was a building occupying a relatively

TOP: *King Robert I and his first wife Isabelle of Mar, from a late 16th-century pictorial record of the Scottish royal family.*

ABOVE: *Cast of the great seal of King Robert I.*

FACING PAGE: *Another fine example of the 16th-century tower-house is to be found at Castle Fraser. (See page 32.)*

Castles of Scotland

FRONT COVER: *The magnificent 13th-century castle of Eilean Donan stands on an island at the junction of Lochs Long and Duich. (See page 32.)*

BACK COVER: *Crathes Castle is today 'defended' by extensive gardens containing many beautiful flowers, shrubs and trees. (See page 13.)*

ABOVE: *The massive Clan Maclean stronghold of Duart Castle almost rises out of the cliffs of Duart Bay on the Island of Mull. (See page 32.)*

CASTLES of SCOTLAND

David R. Cook

Introduction

The year 1066 is universally known as the date of the Norman Conquest and the introduction of feudal institutions into England. The most enduring of these institutions was the castle or the fortified residence of the feudal lord. From his castle the lord administered and protected his estates, the source of his wealth and position in society. After the Norman Conquest the castle became an integral part of the English countryside and the cornerstone of the new alien rule. In Scotland the introduction of feudalism and castles was a later and more gradual process. It was not until the 12th century and the reigns of Alexander I (1107–1124) and more particularly his brother David I (1124–1153) that feudal land tenure and castles came to lowland Scotland.

The death of their father Malcolm Canmore in 1093 had led to turmoil in Scotland. His sons had sought refuge in England where they grew up in the feudal world of the Norman court. The effect was evidently greatest on David. When he returned to Scotland he began introducing Norman retainers, feudal landholding and castles. This process of Normanization was greatly expanded when David succeeded his brother as king in 1124.

As in England, the first castles built north of the border were of the motte-and-bailey variety. The basic reason was undoubtedly the ease of construction. The motte was a high mound of earth, shaped like a truncated cone, with a circular, flat top. A ditch surrounded the mound, providing material for the latter. At the foot of the motte lay one or more baileys, usually kidney-shaped and also surrounded by a ditch which joined that round the motte. The soil thrown up from this ditch was used to make a rampart along the edge of the bailey. The summit of the motte was crowned by a wooden tower or donjon, the residence of the feudal lord. In the bailey there were other wooden buildings for the garrison and their horses.

The geographical distribution of the surviving mottes in Scotland shows that by far their greatest concentration is to be found in the south-west between the Clyde and the Solway. There is a less dense but appreciable number of mottes in central Scotland and north from the river Forth to the coast of the Moray Firth. They are, however, quite scarce in the Highlands. This pattern of distribution largely corresponds with the known geographical extent of the process of feudalization begun in the 12th

century by the Canmore dynasty. By introducing and then strengthening feudal ties and landholding, and erecting royal castles, these kings reasserted the power of the monarchy in the same way as the Norman kings had done in England. Surviving mottes in towns like Lanark, Peebles and Elgin probably represent the earliest remains of royal administrative castles associated with the establishment of royal burghs and sheriffdoms. These royal burghs were either founded by the king or established a special relationship with him. In return for trading privileges and various rights of self-government, the burghs made generous contributions to the royal finances. The sheriff was a royal servant who supervised the collection of the local royal dues and rents and who held the royal castle. He was not, as in England, the administrator of the shire court for such courts did not exist in Scotland.

However, only a relatively small proportion of the surviving mottes are found in known areas of direct royal control. They are much more numerous in regions like the semi-independent principality of Galloway where royal authority was less clearly established. Malcolm IV (1153–1165) is known to have launched at least three expeditions into Galloway and he may well have erected many of the mottes there in order to establish his authority firmly over that troublesome area. Therefore these primitive but highly effective castles represented the potent military element in royal authority. Indeed they proved so effective that some overmighty subjects began to build their own motte-and-bailey castles to counter royal power. One such was Roland, the penultimate native Lord of Galloway, at the end of the 12th century.

The timber construction of the more important motte-and-bailey castles began to give way to building in stone and lime from around the beginning of the 13th century. Many of the others may have continued in use until the later Middle Ages with comparatively little structural development. Their military effectiveness obviously declined but they remained important

small ground-surface area in relation to its volume, forming a tall narrow structure in which the main apartments were piled one above the other. Nowhere did the tower-house achieve such popularity as in late-medieval Scotland, where it far outnumbered all other forms of fortified baronial residence. Indeed the tower-house is the archetypal Scottish castle. The reasons for its popularity are not difficult to fathom. Few Scottish barons of the period had either the means or the necessity to indulge in the building of major castles. Therefore they erected less grandiose but more economic tower-houses. Their individual sizes varied according to the means and requirements of each particular lord. A border-lord would place a greater emphasis on defence, others on residential aspects, but in general the tower-house was able to strike an appropriate balance between the two. Superficially similar to the 12th-century Norman keeps, the military requirements of the Scottish tower-house were very different. It was not designed to withstand a full-

scale siege but to resist a sudden assault by a local skirmishing party.

The earliest towers, erected during the 13th and 14th centuries, were usually of a simple rectangular plan. More complex structures with ancillary wings, often forming an 'L' or 'Z' shaped plan, became increasingly common as the years passed by. In the simple rectangular tower the accommodation usually comprised a ground-floor cellar, a hall at first-floor level, and one or more upper storeys. The walls were usually bound together and strengthened by massive stone buttresses, while in the interests of defence the entrance was often found at first-floor level.

The later towers were less massively constructed. They underwent considerable development in the 16th century after a temporary pause in the years following the battle of Flodden (1513) when many of the castle builders were killed. As the influence of European, and particularly French, styles became felt through the French connections of the Stuart kings of Scotland and the lords

sought more domestic comfort, the tower-house underwent far-reaching changes. Defensive characteristics gradually disappeared or were converted into ornamental features. More fundamentally, the demands of improved residential accommodation led to the tower-house being extended horizontally thus altering the original concept of its design. By the time of the union of the crowns, the tower-house, after dominating baronial residences architecturally for more than three centuries, had begun to be superseded by a new type of residence – the laird's house of the 17th century.

Nevertheless, such buildings have been labelled 'castle' by both contemporaries and subsequent generations of residents and visitors. The word has indeed become overworked in Scotland. That is not to detract from the beauty and comforts of country mansions, such as Culzean Castle, or indeed in the splendid urban residences which characterise recent centuries and make Edinburgh and other Scottish cities a delight to visit.

Balmoral (Grampian)

8 m (13 km) W of Ballater on A93
Tel: Crathie (013397) 42334/5
Owned by Her Majesty The Queen

The immense castellated mansion of Balmoral is set in the gently wooded countryside of the river Dee. Robert II had a hunting lodge here, then Sir Malcolm Drummond built a tower on the same site. The Gordon Earls of Huntly bought the estate in the 15th century and it subsequently changed hands in 1662 and 1798. In *c.*1845 Queen Victoria and Prince Albert paid their first visit to Balmoral, which was at that time leased by Sir Robert Gordon from the Earl of Fife. Queen Victoria declared it was a 'pretty little castle in the old Scotch style'.

Prince Albert paid £31,500 for the 24,000-acre estate and collaborated with an Aberdeen architect, William Smith, to create a picturesque, neo-Gothic mansion in white granite. The prince supervised every detail, including carpets and curtains, and designed a Balmoral tartan for the Royal Family's exclusive use. Queen Victoria found Balmoral a 'dear paradise' and it remains the Royal Family's favourite Scottish retreat today.

Blair (Tayside)

8 m (13 km) NW of Pitlochry on A9
Tel: Blair Atholl (01796) 481207
Owned by the Duke of Atholl

Blair Castle has undergone many changes, expanding and improving with the fortunes of the Atholl family, since it was first built around Comyn's Tower in 1269. By the time Mary Queen of Scots stayed here in 1564, this early tower had been extended southwards to include a great hall.

During the Civil War, the Royalist castle was captured by Cromwell's troops, and continuing Atholl loyalty to the crown was rewarded in 1703 when Queen Anne created the 2nd marquess Duke of Atholl. During the Jacobite rebellion of 1745–46 Blair was the last private castle in Britain to be besieged when Lord George Murray, who had forfeited his inheritance by supporting Bonnie Prince Charlie, laid siege to his own home.

By 1758, the 2nd duke had remodelled the castle as a Georgian mansion, but in 1869 the architect Sir David Bryce restored the medieval appearance. Throughout history, Blair Castle has received many famous guests – such as Edward III, James V, Mary Queen of Scots, Bonnie Prince Charlie, Queen Victoria, and Napoleon III's Empress Eugènie.

Blair has an impressive collection of Sèvres porcelain, Chippendale and Sheraton furniture, and Holbein, Lely and de Witt family portraits. It is owned by the present duke, who is still the head of the famous Atholl Highlanders – the only private army in Britain.

★

ABOVE: *Queen Victoria's 'dear paradise', the royal castle of Balmoral stands in its picturesque grounds on the banks of the Dee. The rare conifers and trees were planted by her beloved Prince Albert.*

FACING PAGE, ABOVE: *The last private castle to be besieged in Britain, Blair Castle is today a sumptuous stately home, beautifully maintained and furnished with treasures and relics from many centuries.*

FACING PAGE, BELOW: *The Tea Room at Blair, which with the other rooms on view presents a picture of Scottish life from the 16th century to the present day. Some exquisite furniture and part of the superb china collection are shown here, while other treasures include family portraits, arms and armour, and toys.*

Braemar (Grampian)

0.5 m (0.8 km) N of Braemar on A93
Tel: Braemar (013397) 41219
Owned by Captain A. A. C. Farquharson
of Invercauld

Braemar Castle was originally built by the Earls of Mar in the 17th century to reinforce their control of the region and it was in 1628 that John Erskine, Earl of Mar, commissioned the L-shaped tower-house. The property was burned out by the enemy clan leader, the legendary Black Colonel, John Farquharson of Inverey after the Glorious Revolution of 1688.

Two years after the devastating defeat of the clans at Culloden, in 1748, Braemar Castle was rebuilt to accommodate English soldiers brought in to enforce the Disarming Act which cruelly prepared the Highlands for the Clearances and the final crushing of all clansmen. The remarkable star-shaped curtain wall was added, so that all angles could be covered by the garrison firing through the many gun-loops.

Visitors can still see the names carved in wooden casements left by the English troops, as well as the pit-prison, the old iron yett (gate), and the crenellated towers.

Brodick (Strathclyde)

On the Isle of Arran
Tel: Brodick (01770) 302202
Owned by the National Trust for Scotland

Brodick Castle stands on the northern shore of Brodick Bay on the beautiful Isle of Arran. It was the seat of the Dukes of Hamilton and latterly the Duke of Montrose until 1958 when it passed to the National Trust for Scotland. Built on the site of a Viking stronghold, the castle dates in part from the 13th century. It was greatly extended in 1652 and 1844. Brodick was three times sacked by English troops. The last military occupation of the castle was at the command of Oliver Cromwell, in the middle of the 17th century. The garrison was later massacred by the islanders.

The castle was renovated in sumptuous style in 1844 when the 11th Duke of Hamilton married Princess Marie of Baden. There are paintings to be seen from the famous Beckford and Hamilton collections as well as magnificent silver and porcelain, and the drawing room has a rich plaster ceiling with various coats of arms.

The grounds have been designated a Country Park and a Ranger Service is offered to the public. To the east of the castle is a magnificent walled garden in Victorian style, and the woodland areas boast a fine collection of rhododendrons which are deservedly world famous.

*

ABOVE: *The romantic Isle of Arran reveals many fine sights and Brodick Castle is comparable with any of them. Robert Bruce fled to Brodick after his defeat at Methven in 1306 to rally support against the English.*

FACING PAGE: *The 17th-century castle at Braemar. The star-shaped curtain wall, with its many gun-loops, is clearly visible.*

Caerlaverock (Dumfries and Galloway)

7 m (11 km) SE of Dumfries on B725
Tel: Glencaple (01387) 770244
In the care of Historic Scotland

Caerlaverock Castle is one of the best surviving examples of medieval castle-building not just in Scotland but in Britain as a whole. An earlier rectangular castle, dating from the early 13th century, lies a few hundred yards away in the woods, but it is now clear that it is the existing castle built *c.*1280, which Edward I besieged and captured during his Scottish campaign of 1300. A contemporary poem describes it as follows: 'In shape it was like a shield, for it had but three sides round it, with a tower at each corner, but one of them was a double one, so high, so deep and so wide, that the gate was underneath it, well made and strong, with a drawbridge and a sufficiency of

other defences. And it had good walls, and good ditches filled right up to the brim with water.' Though ruined, the castle looks very much the same today.

Edward I entrusted the castle to Sir Eustace Maxwell, but in 1313 he declared for Robert Bruce rather than for the pathetic son of the 'hammer of the Scots', Edward II. He subsequently dismantled the castle in accordance with the Scottish policy of rendering useless any stronghold which might prove of strategic value to the English. In spite of this dismantling and several later sieges and reconstructions, much of the original masonry remains, providing an excellent example of the Edwardian style of gatehouse. The splendid east range, with its fine Renaissance façade, was added in the 1630s. Unfortunately it was not to last for long, for the castle was besieged, captured and dismantled by the Covenanters

(Scottish Presbyterians opposed to the introduction of a new Prayer Book by Charles I into his northern kingdom) in 1640.

Castle Fraser (See page 32)

★

ABOVE: *The fine twin-towered gatehouse at the Edwardian castle of Caerlaverock. The castle is triangular in plan and one of the two drum towers at the other angles is clearly visible. Caerlaverock provides the best example in Scotland of the tendency in the late 13th century to concentrate the defensive strength of the castle in the gatehouse.*

FACING PAGE: *This beautiful summer's day scene at Cawdor Castle seems a long way from witches and murder, but the castle is most famous for its involvement in Shakespeare's 'Macbeth'. The powerful central tower is the earliest part of the castle and dates from the 14th century.*

Cawdor *(Highlands)*

4 m (6.4 km) SW of Nairn, off B9090
Tel: Cawdor (01667) 404615
Owned by the Earl of Cawdor, FSA FRICS

Cawdor Castle is famous for its associations with Shakespeare's *Macbeth*. The Thanedom of Cawdor was promised to Macbeth by the witches, and people like to imagine that the castle was the setting for the murder of Duncan. However, none of the castle dates from Macbeth's time in the middle of the 11th century.

In 1454 King James II of Scotland granted a licence to the Thane of Cawdor, permitting him to erect and fortify his castle 'with walls and ditches and equip the summit with turrets and means of defence, with warlike provisions and strengths'. There was an added condition that the castle must always be ready for use by the king and his successors. The central five-storey tower is earlier, *c.*1370, and is surrounded by buildings from the 17th century, which were enlarged and remodelled during the following century.

Craigievar (Grampian)
26 m (42 km) W of Aberdeen, off A980
Tel: Lumphanan (013398) 83635
Owned by the National Trust for Scotland

This beautiful castle, completed in 1626 by the prosperous laird William Forbes, nicknamed 'Willie the Merchant', is one of the five Castles of Mar that comprise the baronial summit of the Scottish castellated style. Until it was presented to the National Trust for Scotland in 1963 it was occupied by direct descendants of William Forbes, the last of whom was the 19th Baron Sempill. Indeed one of the great attractions of the castle is its family atmosphere, very different from the massive royal strongholds of lowland Scotland.

The castle is a tall 'L'-shaped tower-house which, apart from the Georgian sash windows and slate roofs, retains its 17th-century features including gargoyles, corbelling (projecting tiers of stones), turrets and cap houses opening on to the roof. Decorative plaster ceilings, dating from 1625 and 1626 portray biblical and mythical characters. In the hall the Stuart Arms appear above the Italianate chimneypiece. There is a single entrance to the castle, but several stairs, including the secret escape route of the laird, give access to the hall from the top of the building.

Crathes (Grampian)
14 m (22 km) SW of Aberdeen, off A93
Tel: Crathes (01330) 844525
Owned by the National Trust for Scotland

This area north of the river Dee was known as the Lands of Leys and, together with the Horn of Leys (a jewelled ivory horn now located in the main hall of the castle), was granted to Alexander Burnett by Robert Bruce in 1323. The castle was built between 1553 and 1594 and, along with Craigievar, displays many of the best features of the Scottish tower-house.

Crathes is 'L'-shaped with many decorative turrets and dormer windows. By the middle of the 16th century the need for military strength had declined and the builders were free to concentrate rather more on the aesthetics of their work. Crathes is well known for the quality of its painted ceilings, in the Chamber of the Nine Muses and the supposedly haunted Green Lady's Room, and most spectacularly in the Chamber of the Nine Nobles. The Long Gallery has an oak-panelled ceiling with heraldic carvings unique in Scotland.

In 1951 Sir James Burnett presented the castle to the National Trust for Scotland. The gardens contain an outstanding collection of trees and shrubs. The yew hedges date from 1702 and there are four nature trails.

FACING PAGE, ABOVE: *Craigievar Castle is possibly Scotland's finest example of a 17th-century tower-house.*

FACING PAGE, BELOW: *The Hall at Craigievar has a magnificent Renaissance plaster ceiling and a majestic fireplace surmounted by the Stuart Arms.*

ABOVE: *Crathes Castle is renowned for the quality of its painted ceilings. An external view of the castle is on the back cover.*

BELOW: *The Horn of Leys.*

Culzean *(Strathclyde)*

12 m (19 km) SW of Ayr on A719
Tel: Kirkoswald (01655) 760274
Owned by the National Trust for Scotland

Culzean Castle and country park add considerably to the golfing and scenic attractions of Ayrshire, but it is altogether another matter whether the building actually merits the title 'castle'. It was built by Robert Adam for the Kennedy family between 1777 and 1792, replacing an earlier tower-house. Within a few years of the building's completion, the local parish minister described it as follows: 'This noble edifice is situated upon a rock, projecting a little into the sea, of about 100 feet in height from the surface of the water and almost perpendicular ... and such is the style of architecture, such the execution of the work, and the beauty of the stone, that it impresses the mind with delightful ideas of elegance, order and magnificence exceeding anything similar in the country.'

Built in an ostentatiously Italianate style, Culzean is an impressive structure. Of particular interest are the magnificent oval staircase, the round drawing room and the plaster ceilings now restored to Adam's original colouring. In 1945 Culzean was given by the Kennedy family to the National Trust for Scotland. As a tribute to his achievements in World War II, General (later President) Eisenhower was given the top floor flat for the duration of his lifetime. In 1969 the grounds were declared Scotland's first country park.

Dirleton *(Lothian)*

16 m (26 km) NW of Edinburgh on A198
Tel: Dirleton (01620) 850330
In the care of Historic Scotland

This ruin stands beside a flower-garden in one of Scotland's most picturesque villages. In the 12th century the Anglo-Norman family of de Vaux acquired the barony of Dirleton and they built the original stone castle. It was one of the most formidable Scottish castles of its time and was believed to be impervious to the stone-throwing siege engines of the 13th century. Nevertheless Bishop Anthony Bek of Durham successfully besieged the castle in 1298. The English held it until 1311 when it was recovered by the army of Robert Bruce. Parts of the fabric were probably dismantled in accordance with the usual policy of rendering useless any stronghold which might prove of value to the English.

In 1382 the castle and barony of Dirleton passed to the Halyburton family. Throughout the 14th and 15th centuries, members of the family were responsible for repairing and extending the castle buildings to include the vaults, great hall and the remodelled entrance. In 1515, the castle and one third of the barony passed to the Ruthven family who showed themselves to be equally energetic in adding to the castle's buildings. The Ruthvens were very active in the politics of the 16th century, and were involved in the murder of Riccio, Mary Queen of Scots' favourite, in 1566 and the Gowrie Conspiracy of 1600, in which two members of the family lost their lives in an alleged attempt to murder James VI.

In 1650 Cromwell's troops occupied and ruined the castle.

FACING PAGE: *Robert Adam's lavish Italianate staircase at Culzean Castle.*

ABOVE: *Culzean is one of Robert Adam's most outstanding achievements, whether in the fountains, ponds, trees and shrubs of the gardens or the sumptuous residence built for the Kennedy family in the late 18th century. The castle is now maintained by the National Trust for Scotland.*

BELOW: *Dirleton Castle has seen many additions since it was first constructed in the 12th century, but it has been in ruins since Cromwell's troops ransacked it in 1650. Today the castle forms an integral part of one of Scotland's most attractive villages.*

15

ABOVE, LEFT: *The Great Hall at Edinburgh Castle is of early 15th-century origin, but was extensively rebuilt by James IV early in the 16th century. The most interesting feature is the great hammer-beam roof with human and animal masks at the ends of the beams and carved stone corbels supporting them.*

BELOW, LEFT: *The famous artillery piece 'Mons Meg' at the castle dates from the 15th century and was probably forged at Mons in Belgium. It was undoubtedly used at the sieges of Threave Castle (1455) and the English castle of Norham (1497), but it was much less effective in 1682, bursting while firing a salute in honour of the Duke of York, later the Stuart King James II of England.*

ABOVE: *The dramatic and imposing castle site at Edinburgh has probably been fortified since the Iron Age, though the present buildings date from the reign of Malcolm Canmore (1085–1093).*

RIGHT: *The Crown Room at the Castle contains the 'Honours of Scotland' – the royal crown, sceptre and sword. The crown is made of Scottish gold and is decorated with 94 pearls, 10 diamonds and over 30 other stones. It may date from Bruce's reign but was refashioned by James V in the 16th century. The sceptre was a gift from the Borgia Pope, Alexander VI, to James IV. The sword was presented to the same king by another Pope, Julius II.*

17

Doune (Central)

9 m (14.4 km) NW of Stirling, off A84
Tel: Edinburgh (0131) 668 8600 (during office hours)
In the care of Historic Scotland

Doune Castle is one of the largest and best-preserved examples of 14th-century military architecture in Scotland. It was built in a highly strategic position commanding two major routes in medieval Scotland: from Edinburgh to Inverlochy and the west, and from Glasgow to Inverness. The triangular site is naturally well defended, being protected on two sides by the Teith and Ardoch. On the third side is a deep moat. The castle was built by Robert, Duke of Albany (died 1419) and his son, Murdoch (executed in 1425 by King James I) and comprises a powerful curtain wall enclosing a large court dominated by the square gatehouse-tower.

Doune is similar to contemporary castles in England, such as Bodiam in Sussex, in having a gatehouse-tower that formed a self-contained defensive residence. Powerful late-medieval barons, like the Duke of Albany, no chances on the loyalty of their mercenary garrisons. After Murdoch's execution in 1425 the castle was forfeited to the crown, and later James IV gave it to his queen, Margaret. Her third husband was Lord Methven, a descendant of the Dukes of Albany, and the office of constable of the castle became hereditary in his family, the Earls of Moray.

ABOVE: *The 14th-century castle at Doune has been described as 'the highest achievement of perfected castellar construction'. It occupies a triangular site and is dominated by the gatehouse-tower.*

LEFT: *James Stewart, Earl of Moray (1531–70), whose family held the hereditary office of constable of Doune Castle.*

FACING PAGE, ABOVE: *Deep in the beautiful Nithsdale area of south-west Scotland lies Drumlanrig Castle, the 17th-century home of the Dukes of Buccleuch and Queensberry. It is built of local pink sandstone in the shape of a hollow square with imposing corner turrets.*

FACING PAGE, BELOW: *The powerful 13th-century tower at Drum dominates the mansion constructed by the 9th Laird in 1619. This reflects their differing roles: the former was built for defence, while the Renaissance laird was more concerned with his own creature comforts.*

Drum (Grampian)

10 m (16 km) W of Aberdeen, off A93
Tel: Drumoak (01330) 811204
Owned by the National Trust for Scotland

The powerful square tower-house at Drum was built in the late 13th century. In 1323 Drum was granted by Robert Bruce to his standard-bearer, William de Irwyn. The castle remained in the possession of the Irvine family until 1975 when it was bequeathed to the National Trust for Scotland. The tower now stands as one side of a courtyard; in 1619 the 9th Laird added the very impressive Renaissance mansion.

The extensive grounds include nature trails, woodland walks and a garden of historic roses.

Drumlanrig *(Dumfries and Galloway)*

3 m (4.8 km) N of Thornhill, off A76
Tel: Thornhill (01848) 331682
Owned by the Duke of Buccleuch and Queensberry, KT

Originally the site of a 14th-century Douglas stronghold, the present castle was constructed between 1679 and 1691 probably by Robert Mylne, the King's Master Mason, for William Douglas, the 1st Duke of Queensberry. Built in local pink sandstone, it is a fine example of Scottish domestic architecture. The splendid rooms contain paintings by da Vinci, Rembrandt, Holbein, Murillo, Gainsborough and Rowlandson. The family portraits, covering a period of some 300 years, are by Kneller, Reynolds and Ramsay. The beautiful French furniture includes a cabinet presented to Charles II by Louis XIV. Charles later gave it to his son, the Duke of Monmouth and Buccleuch.

Duart *(See page 32)*

Dunrobin *(Highland)*
0.5 m (0.8 km) NE of Golspie on A9
Tel: Golspie (01408) 633177
Owned by the Sutherland Trust

The ancestral seat of the Dukes and Earls of Sutherland, Dunrobin was originally built in the late 13th century by Robert, 2nd Earl of Sutherland. It was dominated by the massive square keep which survives today. Sir Charles Barry, the architect of the Houses of Parliament, completely redesigned the castle during the period 1835–50, creating a highly imaginative baronial residence. In 1915, while in use as a naval hospital, the castle was badly damaged by fire but it was subsequently restored to Barry's design by Sir Robert Lorimer who also contributed a library and several new rooms.

Dunrobin Castle contains a fine collection of paintings, furniture and tapestries, and the magnificent formal gardens are retained in their original Victorian design.

Dunvegan *(Highland)*
On the Isle of Skye
Tel: Dunvegan (01470) 521206
Owned by John MacLeod of MacLeod

Dunvegan Castle has been the ancestral seat of the MacLeods of MacLeod for over 700 years and still remains their home. The name Dunvegan is thought to refer to an earlier time when the Vikings held sway over the Hebrides. The Fairy Tower, the old curtain wall, the dungeon and the original sea-gate (at one time the only entrance) are remnants of earlier centuries of MacLeod building. However, much work was undertaken during the 17th, 18th and 19th centuries and this has tended to change the castle and mask the original medieval appearance.

Some interesting relics are displayed at Dunvegan, including the celebrated Fairy Flag, the Dunvegan Cup, Rory Mor's Horn, and a lock of Bonnie Prince Charlie's hair.

FACING PAGE, ABOVE: *Dunrobin Castle, the ancestral home of the Dukes and Earls of Sutherland, stands majestically on a natural terrace overlooking Dornoch Firth. The first castle was a square keep with angle turrets. Various additions followed until Sir Charles Barry restored Dunrobin as a lavish stately home.*

FACING PAGE, BELOW: *After the fire of 1915 Dunrobin was restored to its former glory by Sir Robert Lorimer. Probably his finest achievement is the magnificent library.*

ABOVE: *The famous seat of the Clan MacLeod, Dunvegan Castle, lies in the north-west corner of the Isle of Skye. Many MacLeod relics are on display, including the Fairy Flag. Made of silk woven in Syria or Rhodes and possibly as old as the 7th century, the Flag has the power to save the MacLeods from destruction on three occasions – to date it has been unfurled twice.*

Edinburgh (Lothian)

Tel: Edinburgh (0131) 225 9847
In the care of Historic Scotland

The castle stands 443 ft (135 m) above sea level on a plug of volcanic rock. The buildings range in date from the 12th-century St. Margaret's Chapel to the 20th-century Scottish National War Memorial. It is known the site was fortified in the Iron Age but its royal history begins with the reign of Malcolm Canmore (1058–1093) who made Edinburgh his principal residence. He married Margaret, the great-niece of Edward the Confessor, who became renowned for her piety and charity and was later canonized. The little chapel that bears her name has stood on the rock through nearly eight and a half centuries of Scottish history. Margaret died in the castle in November 1093, after hearing of the death in battle of her husband and her eldest son.

The castle was captured in 1313 by the Scottish army led by the Earl of Moray, the nephew of Robert Bruce. Moray with only thirty men scaled the rock and the walls at midnight, overpowered the English garrison and took the castle. In accordance with Bruce's policy of rendering ineffective any stronghold which the English might use against him, Moray had the castle dismantled. Time and again, as the Anglo-Scottish wars wore on, Edinburgh changed hands. It suffered considerable damage but repairs and alterations were continually being carried out. Today only the ruin of David's Tower dates from the defences built before the 15th century. The subsequent rebuilding of the 16th and 17th centuries showed a marked accent on the residential aspects of the castle. This is clearly seen in the main buildings such as the palace and the great hall.

Yet the castle still retained an importance as a military stronghold. The powerful approach to its heart beneath Half Moon Battery and through Portcullis Gate, was constructed in the late 16th century. During the Civil War the castle surrendered to Cromwell after a three-month bombardment in 1650. It surrendered again in 1689,

ABOVE: *St. Margaret's Chapel was probably built by Margaret, the wife of Malcolm Canmore, though it may have been founded later in her honour by her son, David I.*

BELOW: *Bonnie Prince Charlie besieged the castle in autumn 1745, but, as with most things in his life, he failed. After Culloden he fled into exile, eventually dying in Rome. He is buried in the crypt of St. Peter's, unaware that the marble monument was partly paid for by the Hanoverian George III.*

FACING PAGE, ABOVE: *The Edinburgh military tattoo is held on the Castle Esplanade during the Festival. The Esplanade is also the scene for the ancient ceremony of Beating the Retreat in May and June.*

FACING PAGE, BELOW: *The outer gateway into the castle. Statues of Robert Bruce and William Wallace, the two great patriots of the Wars of Independence, flank the entrance.*

this time to William of Orange after holding out for the last Stuart king, James II. The final defence was in 1745, when Bonnie Prince Charlie, marching south with his Highlanders to the battle of Prestonpans, occupied Edinburgh from 22 September to 31 October and blockaded the castle. They soon realized they could not take the castle. Within a year many of them found themselves prisoners there following the collapse of their cause at the bloody battle of Culloden (16 April 1746). Since then Edinburgh Castle, indeed Scotland, has rested at peace.

The castle continued as a prison for French soldiers until the end of the Napoleonic Wars. Since then many British monarchs have visited this famous site of so much of Scotland's dramatic history and, fittingly, the castle was chosen to enshrine the Scottish National War Memorial in the wake of the First World War.

Eilean Donan *(See page 32)*

Floors *(Borders)*
1 m (1.6 km) NW of Kelso on A6089
Tel: Kelso (01573) 223333
Owned by the Duke of Roxburghe

Similar to Culzean in really being a stately home rather than a castle, Floors is the ancestral seat of the Dukes of Roxburghe. It was built by Robert Adam's father, William, in the years 1721–1725. This renowned family of Scottish-born architects built in a style that was basically Roman and Italian rather than native. However, Floors was extended and given most of its present appearance by William Playfair in the middle of the 19th century.

Floors is said to be the largest inhabited mansion in Scotland and contains splendid furnishings, tapestries and paintings. In the castle grounds a holly tree marks the spot where Scotland lost one of her more able kings. James II besieged the English-held Roxburgh Castle in 1460. A great enthusiast for artillery, he was too close to one of his cannons when it exploded.

Glamis *(Tayside)*
5 m (8 km) SW of Forfar, off A928
Tel: Glamis (01307) 840242
Owned by the Earl of Strathmore and Kinghorne

Glamis Castle is the imposing and historic home of the Earls of Strathmore and Kinghorne. The castle owes its present appearance, with its numerous turrets and battlements, to the 17th century and principally the efforts of the 3rd Earl of Strathmore. However, parts of the 'L' shaped tower date from the 15th century.

There has in fact been a building here from the early middle ages. King Malcolm II is said to have been murdered in or near the castle in 1034. When Lady Glamis was burned for witchcraft and conspiring to murder James V in 1537, the castle was forfeited to the crown, though when her innocence had been established, it was restored to her son and the Strathmore family has held it ever since.

Today the castle, with its close ties to the royal family, is a popular tourist attraction. There is much to see in the castle and grounds. Of note are Duncan's Hall, the oldest part of the castle, and the King Malcolm Room, so named because traditionally the king died here. The grounds include a late 19th-century formal garden and an Italian garden.

★

FACING PAGE, ABOVE: *The sumptuous internal decor and lavish furnishings of the Roxburghe residence at Floors are perfectly illustrated here in the magnificent Drawing Room.*

FACING PAGE, BELOW: *The daffodils add a touch of spring colour to the façade of Floors Castle.*

ABOVE: *Glamis Castle has very close ties with the royal family. It was the childhood home of Queen Elizabeth, the Queen Mother, and Princess Margaret was born here in 1930.*

25

Hermitage (Borders)

15 m (24 km) S of Hawick on B6399
Tel: Edinburgh (0131) 668 8600 (during office hours)
In the care of Historic Scotland

No precise date is given for the building of Hermitage Castle, though records show that a castle was in existence in the late 13th century. Edward I ordered its repair in 1300 at a cost of £20. The earliest owners were the de Soulis family, hereditary King's Butlers of Scotland, one of whom, according to legend, was wrapped in lead and boiled in a cauldron on the Nine Stane rig. Indeed, this brooding castle was the scene of many violent feuds and border skirmishes.

The earliest parts of the present 'H'-shaped building have been dated to the middle of the 14th century. The Douglases built the great central block and the powerful corner towers. Then the castle passed to the Dacre family, the Hepburn Earls of Bothwell and later to the Scotts of Buccleuch. Mary Queen of Scots made her historic ride from Jedburgh to Hermitage when her lover the Earl of Bothwell lay wounded in the castle in 1566, a round trip of approximately 55 miles (88 km) over the hills in mid-October. By the 18th century the castle was in ruins but it was extensively repaired by the Duke of Buccleuch in 1820.

Sir Walter Scott considered Hermitage his favourite castle and had his portrait painted by Raeburn for his friend Constable with Hermitage as a background.

Huntly (See page 32)

★

ABOVE: *The border stronghold of Hermitage Castle still conveys an air of massive impregnability. Today's ruin is mainly from the 14th century and comprises a powerful keep and corner towers, joined by great arches at the eastern and western ends.*

BELOW: *Raeburn's portrait of Sir Walter Scott with Hermitage in the background.*

FACING PAGE: *The fine Gothic-style façade of Inverary Castle conceals magnificently-decorated Georgian rooms.*

Inveraray (Strathclyde)

Tel: Inveraray (01499) 302203
Owned by the Trustees of the 10th Duke of Argyll

The castle of Inveraray, the seat of the Duke of Argyll, head of Clan Campbell, is situated on the north-west border of Loch Fyne amidst some of the finest highland scenery. The old castle, built by Colin Campbell about 1415, was situated only 80 yards (73 metres) from the present castle but it was swept away, as was the nearby town, in the grand scheme of rebuilding carried out by Roger Morris and Robert Mylne in the middle of the 18th century for the 3rd and 5th Dukes.

The castle is built of blue-grey chlorite slate quarried at Creggans on Loch Fyne. It is one of the earliest examples of Gothic revival architecture, the garden front being the most complete and attractive example of the style. The medieval character was achieved through the round towers, the lance-headed windows and arches, the decorative stone palisading and the baronial keep in the courtyard. Whereas the exterior was largely the work of Morris, Mylne was responsible for the rich neo-classical interior decorations.

The castle houses an outstanding collection of furniture, paintings and porcelain, and some interesting early Scottish weapons. After fire damage to the roof in the 1870s, the corner towers were topped with tall conical slate roofs.

TOP: *The rocky-looking ruined castle of St. Andrews dates chiefly from the 16th century, though the site has been fortified since c. 1200.*

LEFT: *As at Edinburgh, nature has provided formidable defences for Stirling Castle.*

ABOVE: *Mary Queen of Scots (1547–87).*

FACING PAGE: *The Battle of Bannockburn (1314), from John Fordun's 'Scotichronicon' in the 15th century.*

St. Andrews (Fife)

Tel: St. Andrews (01334) 477196
In the care of Historic Scotland

The castle occupies a coastal promontory and is protected on the north and east by the cliffs and sea. On the south and west, the castle was cut off by a deep ditch, the approach to the entrance being by a drawbridge. The castle as it survives today is principally the work of the 14th and 16th centuries, but it overlies and incorporates within its walls parts of earlier work. Documentary evidence indicates that the original castle was built c.1200 by Bishop Roger. Therefore from its foundation the castle was intimately linked with the See of St. Andrews. In the course of time it has served the threefold purpose of episcopal palace, fortress and state prison.

During the Wars of Independence, the castle was captured, recaptured, dismantled and rebuilt by both sides until, after Bannockburn (1314), it was occupied and restored by Bishop William Lamberton (1298–1328), a staunch patriot and supporter of Bruce. By 1336 it was once again in English hands but their tenure proved short-lived. The following year the castle was recaptured by Sir Andrew Moray and then dismantled to avoid the risk of it falling under English control again.

For about fifty years it lay in ruins, until the succession of Bishop Walter Traill (1385–1401). He rebuilt the castle and James I and James II both spent some time at St. Andrews in the 15th century. The latter's son, the future James III, may well have been born here in 1451.

The castle's most turbulent associations are with Cardinal David Beaton (1539–1546), a man of strong Catholic ambitions, who had the Protestant reformer George Wishart burnt to death for heresy here in 1546. The cardinal was himself murdered three months later by a band of Protestants, and his body then hung from a wall-head. The Protestants, with John Knox as their chaplain, were subsequently besieged in the castle for a year until the arrival of a French fleet forced them to surrender. They were taken away by the French and Knox spent the next two years as a galley-slave. A feature of great interest surviving from the siege of 1546–7 is the mine and counter-mine tunnelled through the rock beneath the castle. Discovering that the besiegers were driving a tunnel with the intention of breaching the fortifications in several places, the defenders drove a number of shafts of their own until they succeeded in breaking through to the attackers' tunnel.

Stirling (Central)

Tel: Stirling (01786) 450000
In the care of Historic Scotland

The commanding heights of Stirling Castle dominate the main ford of the Forth, the strategic link between northern and southern Scotland. The castle has appropriately been called the 'key to Scotland'. As a result its possession has been the focus of contention for many centuries, with battles like Bannockburn (1314) being fought in its shadow. After his victory, Bruce dismantled the castle so that the English would not be able to exploit its possession again.

It is therefore difficult to ascertain the date of the earlier castle, though its chapel existed by 1124. The present castle dates mainly from the 15th and 16th centuries when it was a principal royal residence. James III was born here in 1451, James V spent his childhood here, and the infant Mary Queen of Scots was crowned here on 9 September 1543. Work in the 16th century largely shaped the structure as it survives today. Its main features are the central turreted gatehouse with its flanking towers and curtain wall, the Great Hall, the Palace, one of the earliest Renaissance buildings in Scotland, and the Chapel Royal.

29

Tantallon *(See page 32)*

Threave *(Dumfries and Galloway)*
1 m (1.6 km) NW of Castle Douglas, off A75
Tel: Edinburgh (0131) 668 8600 (during office hours)
In the care of Historic Scotland

This 14th-century Douglas stronghold stands on an island in the river Dee. It was built *c.*1360–70 by Archibald the Grim, the bastard son of Sir James Douglas who took the heart of Robert Bruce on a posthumous crusade through Spain. The castle is dominated by Archibald's tower. It stands four storeys high with a large corbel projecting out from the battlements. By tradition this was used by Archibald to hang his many victims, but it more likely supported a machicolated platform defending the entrance beneath.

The strong outer curtain wall with its four cylindrical towers, each containing gunloops, probably dates from 1455 when the castle endured its first long siege. James II had determined on the destruction of the Black Douglases and in 1452 murdered the 8th Earl in Stirling Castle. James Douglas, the 9th and last Earl, openly accused the king of the murder and raised 40,000 men against him. It was all to no avail and the Douglases were defeated at Arkinholm in May 1455. As his other strongholds fell, Earl James granted Threave to the English king in a desperate attempt to save it. However, James II was not going to be denied. He bombarded Threave with his formidable gun 'Mons Meg' until the garrison surrendered.

In 1640 the Covenanters captured and dismantled the castle and during the Napoleonic Wars it was used to house French prisoners. The estate was presented to the National Trust for Scotland in 1948 and it was they who established the

School for Practical Gardening in the Victorian house.

Urquhart (Highland)

16 m (26 km) SW of Inverness on A82
Tel: Drumnadrochit (01456) 450551
In the care of Historic Scotland

Loch Ness was raised 6 ft (1.8 m) when the Caledonian Canal was built by Thomas Telford in 1803–23 and Castle Urquhart now stands 44 ft (13 m) above the level of the loch on a rocky promontory. Its situation must have been quite spectacular before the raising of the level of the water. It was built principally as an observation post, and is now a favourite haunt for would-be spotters of the famous Loch Ness Monster as it commands a view almost from Inverness to Fort Augustus. The site has revealed traces of Iron Age habitation and was probably fortified as early as the 6th century when St. Columba visited the area and apparently encountered a sea creature.

The original castle was built by Alan Durward or De Lundin, brother-in-law of Alexander II. It passed to the Comyn family on his death in 1268 or 1275. During the Wars of Independence it changed hands several times, sustaining damage and being repaired on each occasion. The conflicts between the Scottish Crown and the leading family in the Highlands, the Lords of the Isles, caused Urquhart Castle to become once again the scene of violent strife during which much of the surrounding area was laid waste. The devastation of the later middle ages continued into the 16th century and by 1527 the castle was in ruins.

The ruins which survive today are largely those of the castle as it was rebuilt in the 16th and 17th centuries by the Grant family, who had been first awarded the castle and lordship in 1509 by James IV. In 1692 the castle was blown up by the troops who had occupied it after the Jacobite uprising of 1689, thus preventing it from becoming a Jacobite base at a later date. Since then it has not been occupied. In 1715 a storm blew down the south wall of the already dilapidated 16th-century tower.

FACING PAGE: *Set in its picturesque site on a small island in the River Dee, the old Douglas stronghold of Threave seems an eternity away from civil strife, sieges and artillery bombardment. Yet it was to this quiet and beautiful spot that James II dragged his massive cannon 'Mons Meg' to bombard the castle into submission in 1455. It was the end of the Black Douglases, but not of Threave. Today the castle is in a very fair state of preservation, partly because it was used to house French prisoners during the Napoleonic Wars. It is well worth a visit and the sense of adventure is increased by the boat trip necessary to reach the island.*

ABOVE: *Urquhart Castle is an ideal site for 'monster spotting', occupying a rocky promontory on the northern bank of Loch Ness. Although 'Nessie' only came to modern public notice during the 1930s, it was as long ago as the 6th century that St. Adamnan in his biography of St. Columba recorded a sighting. Over the years there have been several sightings and photographs, and the monster has also been the object of serious scientific investigation utilising modern methods of detection, so far without any decisive result. A principal problem has been the size of the Loch. It is 24 miles long, an average of 1 mile in width and over 900 feet deep in places.*

ABOVE: *Tantallon Castle. (See details below.)*

Other castles pictured in this book:

Castle Fraser *(Grampian)*
(Pictured on page 5)
16 m (26 km) NW of Aberdeen, off A944
Tel: Sauchen (01330) 833463
Owned by the National Trust for Scotland

Building began in about 1575 for the 6th Laird, Michael Fraser, and was completed in 1636. A round seven-storey tower and extensions were added to the earlier keep, making this one of the finest examples of the 'Z' shaped plan.

Duart *(Strathclyde)*
(Pictured on page 1)
On the Isle of Mull
Tel: Craignure (01680) 812309
Owned by Sir Lachlan Maclean, Bt

The foundations of Duart on Mull are 13th-century Norman and parts of the original enclosing wall survive. It has always been the home of the Macleans with one short break, in the aftermath of Culloden, when it was garrisoned by the English. In 1911 Sir Fitzroy Maclean repurchased and restored the castle; it is now lived in by the present chief, Sir Lachlan Maclean.

Eilean Donan *(Highland)*
(Pictured on the front cover)
8 m (13 km) E of Kyle of Lochalsh on A87
Tel: Dornie (01599) 555202
Owned by The Conchra Charitable Trust

Standing on a rocky island at the junction of three lochs and linked to the mainland by a causeway, Eilean Donan originated in 1220 as one of Alexander II's defences against the Danes. It was held by the Jacobites in 1719 and heavily bombarded by an English warship. The castle remained a ruin until 1932 when Colonel MacRae-Gilstrap restored it to its former condition.

Huntly *(Grampian)*
(Pictured on page 3)
Tel: Huntly (01466) 793191
In the care of Historic Scotland

Duncan, Earl of Fife, built a castle on this well-protected site in the late 12th century. It was known as the Peel of Strathbogie and Duncan was the first Laird. During the reign of Robert Bruce the castle was confiscated by the king and given to Sir Adam Gordon of Huntly, Berwickshire. In the 16th century it was renamed Huntly. The imposing ruins of the Renaissance palace built between 1597 and 1602 are all that now remain.

Tantallon *(Lothian)*
3 m (4.8 km) E of North Berwick on A198
Tel: Edinburgh (0131) 668 8600 (during office hours)
In the care of Historic Scotland

The castle stands on a dramatic promontory opposite Bass Rock. The vulnerable landward side is defended by a series of outworks and the powerful curtain wall, with an imposing cylindrical tower at each end and the gatehouse in the middle. The 14th century castle was a Douglas stronghold.

ACKNOWLEDGEMENTS
A. F. Kersting: front cover, pp.15 top, 19 top, 23 bottom; Jarrold, Norwich: pp.1, 24 top; National Library of Scotland: pp.2 (the Duke of Roxburghe), 4 (Sir David Ogilvy); The British Library: p.3 top (MS Add. 35321, f.4b); Derek McDougall Photography: pp.3 bottom, 5; The Trustees of the British Museum: p.4 bottom; Andy Williams Photographic Library: pp.6, 28 top, 31, 32; Woodmansterne Ltd: pp.7 top, bottom (Jeremy Marks), 12 bottom (Nicholas Servian), 13 top and bottom (Clive Friend), 14, 19 bottom (Jeremy Marks), 25 (Jeremy Marks); Ernest J. Cooke: p.8; The Photo Source: pp.9, 26 top, 30; Sonia Halliday Photographs: pp.10, 18 top; Picturepoint Ltd: pp.11, 27, 28 bottom left, back cover; Peter Chèze-Brown: p.12 top; James Davis Photography: p.15 bottom; Historic Buildings and Monuments: pp.16 both, 22 top; John Bethell Photography: pp.16/17; Crown Copyright, HMSO (Edinburgh): p.17 bottom; Private Collection: p.18 bottom; Pix Photos: p.20; Lord Strathnaver: p.21 top; The Pilgrim Press: p.21 bottom; Scottish National Portrait Gallery: p.22 bottom; British Tourist Authority: p.23 top; Roxburghe Estates: p.24 bottom; The Duke of Buccleuch KT: p.26 bottom; Crown Copyright, Victoria and Albert Museum: p.28 bottom right; The Master and Fellows of Corpus Christi College, Cambridge: p.29 (MS171 f.265). Map by Robert Clarke Studio Ltd.